# Fast▶▶
# Forward
## *Maths*

### *Hilary Koll and Steve Mills*

Hodder & Stoughton

A MEMBER OF THE HODDER HEADLINE GROUP

# Acknowledgements

Illustrations by Richard Duszczak, and Ian Foulis & Associates.
Text design by Lynda King.

Orders: please contact Bookpoint Ltd, 78 Milton Park, Abingdon, Oxon OX14 4TD. Telephone: (44) 01235 827720, Fax: (44) 01235 400454. Lines are open from 9.00 – 6.00, Monday to Saturday, with a 24 hour message answering service. Email address: orders@bookpoint.co.uk

*British Library Cataloguing in Publication Data*
A catalogue record for this title is available from The British Library

ISBN 0 340 782005

First published 2000
Impression number    10 9 8 7 6 5 4 3
Year                 2006 2005 2004 2003 2002 2001

Copyright © 2000 Steve Mills and Hilary Koll

Cover artwork by Matthew Cooper, Debut Art
Typeset by Lynda King
Printed in Italy for Hodder & Stoughton Educational, a division of Hodder Headline Plc, 338 Euston Road, London NW1 3BH by Printer Trento.

# CONTENTS

# Introduction for the Teacher

The **Fast Forward Pupils' Book** is a central resource that offers the teacher a sharply focused tool for helping pupils to step up from Level 3 to Level 4 in mathematics. In line with the National Numeracy Strategy, it is designed to be used flexibly as part of an interactive, teacher-led programme.

It is *not* a book for children to work through on their own from start to finish. Experience has shown that this approach fails many children, who, at this age, are simply unable to learn their mathematics solely from text.

Success will depend on the teacher's involvement. Probing, challenging and interacting with pupils to explore the ideas in the book will help to bring the mathematics to life. Time for thinking and discussing, explaining and investigating leads to increased confidence, enthusiasm and understanding.

Each unit of the Pupils' Book has been written to tackle the aspects of Level 4 mathematics that many children find most difficult. Common areas of pupil weakness are addressed through ten units, to correspond with the ten-day summer schools. The focused unit approach can, of course, be effectively used as part of any programme for Level 3/4 children.

**The Fast Forward Teachers' Book** provides a rich source of ideas to extend and develop the materials of the Pupils' Book. Additional information accompanies each unit to extend and enrich the activities. The Teachers' Book contains detailed suggestions for maximising real-life opportunities, including outdoor events, open-ended investigations, puzzles and games. These are particularly important in developing a varied, stimulating and enjoyable programme for summer schools. In addition, photocopiable sheets are included to offer further opportunities for practice and consolidation in school or at home.

# UNIT ONE  Addition and Subtraction

In this unit you will learn:

   ★  the words that mean addition or subtraction
   ★  ways to help you add and subtract numbers in your head
   ★  how to tackle missing number puzzles
   ★  to solve worded problems.

## Warm up – workout!

Warm up your minds! Answer these addition and subtraction questions!

| | | |
|---|---|---|
| 6 + 4 = .......... | 7 + 9 = .......... | 17 + 5 = .......... |
| 22 + 9 = .......... | 27 + 6 = .......... | 45 + 12 = .......... |
| 36 + 8 = .......... | 29 + 13 = .......... | 56 + 19 = .......... |

| | | |
|---|---|---|
| 9 – 6 = .......... | 12 – 7 = .......... | 21 – 9 = .......... |
| 30 – 15 = .......... | 29 – 6 = .......... | 45 – 11 = .......... |
| 33 – 19 = .......... | 100 – 51 = .......... | 45 – 28 = .......... |

Find your answers in the grid and colour them in. What does it say?

| 19 | 49 | 12 | 11 | 18 | 16 | 2 | 22 | 30 |
|----|----|----|----|----|----|----|----|----|
| 57 | 48 | 13 | 75 | 61 | 10 | 14 | 21 | 39 |
| 3 | 8 | 51 | 33 | 13 | 5 | 44 | 43 | 37 |
| 8 | 31 | 15 | 1 | 17 | 42 | 8 | 34 | 23 |

## Facts

### Addition and subtraction

It doesn't matter which way round the numbers in an addition question are, the answer is the same…

| 3 | + | 12 | = 15 |  | 12 | + | 3 | = 15 |

This is not true for subtraction. Try it and see!

## Activity

Look at the addition and subtraction statements above. Where do you find the largest number in addtion statements? What about in subtraction statements?

# Word work

Which of these words mean addition and which mean subtraction?

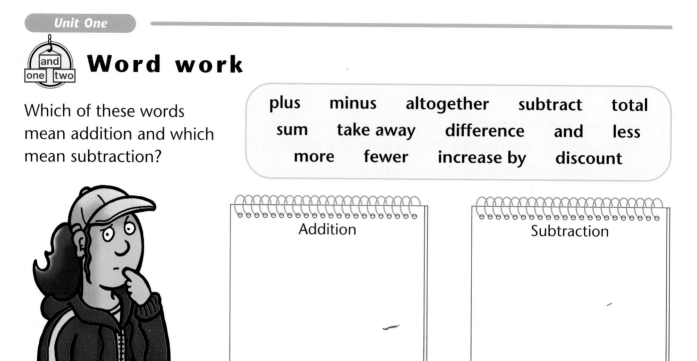

plus   minus   altogether   subtract   total
sum   take away   difference   and   less
more   fewer   increase by   discount

Addition

Subtraction

Sort the words into two groups.

# Skills builder

Jack has a good way of finding the answers to these questions.

The sum of 37 and 25 is 62

37        57   60   62
     20      3    2

The difference between 57 and 38 is 19

38   40       50       57
  2     10      7

Try answering these the same way:

## The Daily News   July 26th 2000

United scored 47 goals before Christmas and 26 after Christmas, making a total of ▢

47

In a survey 62 people went to work by train and 35 drove to work. This is a difference of ▢

35                62

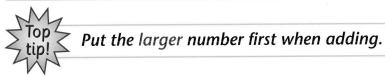

**Top tip!** *Put the larger number first when adding.*

This is Nita's homework.
Tick the correct answers and cross out the wrong ones.

14 and 38 is 62

28 less than 51 is 23

The difference between 43 and 69 is 26

Increasing 23 by 86 gives 119

Decreasing 104 by 47 gives 54

38 _____

_____ 51

43 _____ 69

_____

_____

## ? Question cracker

How quickly can you find these missing numbers?

50 + ◯ = 101     32 + ◯ = 40     ◯ + 20 = 30

12 − ◯ = 6     ◯ − 15 = 20     ◯ − 25 = 50

**Top tips!** *Addition questions can be solved by using subtraction and subtraction questions by using addition.*

*In addition questions the answer will be the largest number.*

*In subtraction the first number will be the largest.*

Use your calculator to solve these questions:

$100 - \boxed{\phantom{XXX}} = 35$

$\boxed{\phantom{XXX}} + 28 = 47$

$\boxed{\phantom{XXX}} - 687 = 128$

$476 + \boxed{\phantom{XXX}} = 762$

$3156 + \boxed{\phantom{XXX}} = 10001$

$\boxed{\phantom{XXX}} + 5756 = 9284$

Arrange the three cards in different ways to make as
many addition and subtraction statements as you can.

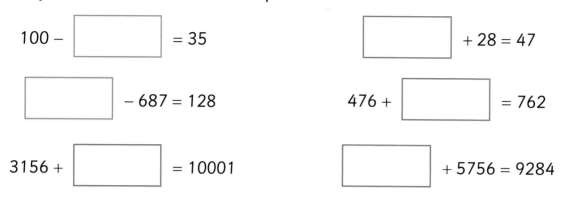

26    45    71

$45 + 26 = 71$

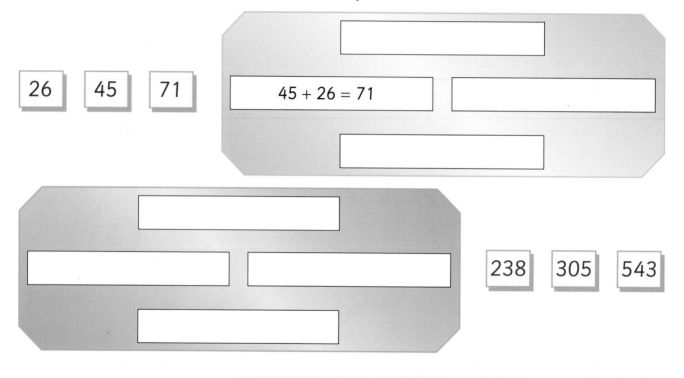

238    305    543

Help the newspaper editor
to finish the headlines :

# MATHS MONTHLY
## all the latest maths news!

August 2000

*Two Great Discoveries Made!!!*

The positions of the largest number in addition and subtraction
statements have been found!!

In addition statements it is always $\boxed{\phantom{XXXXX}}$

In subtraction statements it is always $\boxed{\phantom{XXXXX}}$

# Solve it

Read these headlines and work out the missing numbers.

67 dinner ladies were presented with awards yesterday at Buckingham Palace. Another 24 are to be given awards today, giving _____ altogether.

Local police have reported a decrease in crime in the area. In 1998 there were 82 burglaries. In the following year there was a decrease of 36, with only _____ burglaries in 1999.

**SALE!**
£42 discount on all large-screen TVs.

Original price £410
Sale price _____

**74 players were booked in the Premier League on Saturday, with 48 more on Sunday. This total of _____ is a new record.**

## Talking Points

Look out for where units of measurement are different, such as cm and m, or mm and cm. Change the numbers so that they are all the same unit.

**Increase 3 m by 112 cm.**

Change both to metres          3 m + 1.12 m =

or to centimetres          300 cm + 112 cm =

Jo and Rob are arguing. Tick who is right in each question.

1 m take away 29 cm equals 81 cm

No, it equals 71 cm

133 cm plus 2.5 m is 3.83 m

You're wrong! It's 1.38 m

25 mm and 4.7 cm are 4.95 cm

No! They are 72 mm

If I decrease 3.2 cm by 17 mm I get 1.5 cm

No, you get 3.03 cm

# Game on

Play this game with a friend. You will need a coloured pencil each.
1. Take it in turns to choose a number from each box.
2. You can add or subtract these.
3. If the answer is in the grid, colour it in.

The winner is the first to get four in a line. The line can be horizontal, vertical or diagonal.

| 182 | 210 | 152 | 193 | 128 | 170 |
|-----|-----|-----|-----|-----|-----|
| 17  | 146 | 48  | 47  | 129 | 168 |
| 327 | 51  | 374 | 164 | 35  | 175 |
| 292 | 315 | 34  | 187 | 42  | 150 |
| 229 | 22  | 309 | 30  | 147 | 31  |
| 65  | 133 | 12  | 211 | 28  | 156 |

58   41   64   76   123

106   88   251   92

# Let's investigate

Find the heights of five people. Write them here:

| Name | | | | | |
|--------|--|--|--|--|--|
| Height | | | | | |

★ If these five people lay in a line, head to toe, along the playground, how long would the line be? ...............................

★ Is the line longer than 5 metres? By how much is it longer? ...............................

★ How much shorter than 10 metres is the line? ...............................

---

**Learn these tables facts before starting Unit Two**

| | | | |
|---|---|---|---|
| $3 \times 4 = 12$ | $7 \times 5 = 35$ | $5 \times 9 = 45$ | $6 \times 4 = 24$ |
| $9 \times 0 = 0$ | $6 \times 8 = 48$ | $9 \times 3 = 27$ | $6 \times 7 = 42$ |
| $9 \times 9 = 81$ | $6 \times 6 = 36$ | $9 \times 7 = 63$ | $8 \times 9 = 72$ |

# UNIT TWO   Multiplication

In this unit you will learn:

★ how multiplication works
★ ways to help you multiply in your head and on paper
★ to solve real-life problems with a calculator
★ to solve problems involving money.

## Warm up – workout!

*Cover the page opposite!*

Test yourself on the tables facts from Unit One:

$3 \times 4 =$ ..........    $7 \times 5 =$ ..........

$6 \times 6 =$ ..........    $5 \times 9 =$ ..........

$9 \times 9 =$ ..........    $6 \times 8 =$ ..........

$9 \times 3 =$ ..........    $6 \times 7 =$ ..........

$9 \times 0 =$ ..........    $9 \times 7 =$ ..........

$8 \times 9 =$ ..........    $6 \times 4 =$ ..........

## Remember

It doesn't matter which way round the numbers in a tables fact are, the answer is the same.

$$\boxed{4} \times \boxed{6} = 24 \qquad \boxed{6} \times \boxed{4} = 24$$

All tables facts can be rewritten as division facts, like this:

$$24 \div \boxed{4} = \boxed{6} \quad \text{or} \quad 24 \div \boxed{6} = \boxed{4}$$

Learn the tables facts in the test above as division facts ready for Unit Three.

## Did you know?

You can do the 9 times table on your fingers!
Hold your hands up palms toward you.
For $9 \times 1$ put down your left thumb. How many fingers are still up … 9!
For $9 \times 2$ put down the next finger only.
The thumb to the left is worth 10 and the fingers to the right are worth 1 each … 18!
For $9 \times 3$ put down the third finger only.
The thumb and finger to the left are worth 10 each and the fingers to the right are worth 1 each … 27!

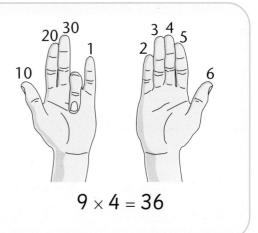

$9 \times 4 = 36$

# Word work

one and two

times    lots of    multiply    groups of
multiplied by    times table    double    halve
product    inverse    multiplication

Bet you can't use each of these words in a maths sentence!

Bet you I can!

Can you ?

.................................................................................. (times)

.................................................................................. (multiplied by)

.................................................................................. (product)

.................................................................................. (double)

.................................................................................. (lots of)

# Skills builder

Look at what happens when we multiply by **10** and **100**.
Let's pick a number to multiply, like 23.

| TTh | Th | H | T | U |
|-----|----|----|----|----|
| | | | 2 | 3 |
| | | 2 | 3 | 0 |
| | 2 | 3 | 0 | 0 |

Start with **23**

$23 \times 10$    digits move one place to the left

$23 \times 100$    digits move two places to the left

Multiply these numbers by 10:    27 ...............    148 ...............

Multiply these numbers by 100:    86 ...............    791 ...............

To multiply by **20**:  just multiply by **2** and then multiply by **10**

$23 \times 20 \longrightarrow 23 \times 2 = 46 \longrightarrow 46 \times 10 = 460$.  So $23 \times 20 = 460$

To multiply by **30**:  just multiply by **3** and then multiply by **10**

$23 \times 30 \longrightarrow 23 \times 3 = 69 \longrightarrow 69 \times 10 = 690$.  So $23 \times 30 = 690$

How would you multiply by 40?

How many pupils will be in the choir?
What would you do to find out?

## The Daily News   July 29th 2000

7 schools will each send 26 pupils to sing in the Schools' Choir.

You can do 26 × 7 like this:

|     | 20  | 6   |       |
| --- | --- | --- | ----- |
| 7   | 140 | 42  | = 182 |

Have a go at these:

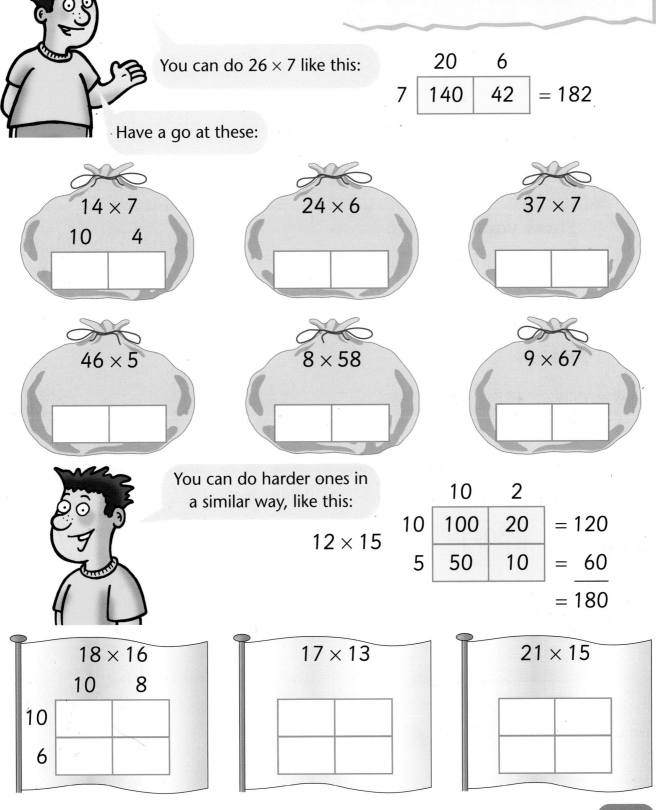

14 × 7

| 10 | 4 |
| --- | --- |
|    |   |

24 × 6

|   |   |
| --- | --- |
|   |   |

37 × 7

|   |   |
| --- | --- |
|   |   |

46 × 5

|   |   |
| --- | --- |
|   |   |

8 × 58

|   |   |
| --- | --- |
|   |   |

9 × 67

|   |   |
| --- | --- |
|   |   |

You can do harder ones in a similar way, like this:

12 × 15

|     | 10  | 2  |       |
| --- | --- | --- | ----- |
| 10  | 100 | 20  | = 120 |
| 5   | 50  | 10  | = 60  |
|     |     |     | = 180 |

18 × 16

|    | 10 | 8 |
| --- | --- | --- |
| 10 |   |   |
| 6  |   |   |

17 × 13

|   |   |
| --- | --- |
|   |   |
|   |   |

21 × 15

|   |   |
| --- | --- |
|   |   |
|   |   |

# Question cracker

### Show your working

Calculate 8 × 53

---

### Show your working

A grocer puts **14 tins** on each shelf.
He has **16 shelves**.
How many **tins** can he have?

---

Answer these questions, giving your answers in pounds.

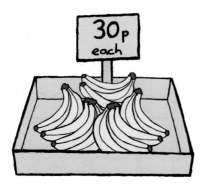

30p
each

Nita buys **8 bananas**.
How much does she spend?

......................................................

99p
for 5

Josh buys **15 apples**.
How much does he pay altogether?

......................................................

### Talking Points    Discuss these with a friend.

**I've found an easy way of multiplying by 5.**

Just **double** the 5 to get 10 and **halve** the other number. It works!

$5 \times 18 =$    **double** 5 to get 10 and **halve** 18 to get 9
double   halve

$10 \times 9 = 90$    so the answer to $5 \times 18 = 90$

Try answering these in the same way:

$5 \times 14 = \boxed{\phantom{00}}$    $5 \times 16 = \boxed{\phantom{00}}$    $24 \times 5 = \boxed{\phantom{00}}$    $28 \times 5 = \boxed{\phantom{00}}$

When the other number is odd, like $5 \times 13$, try this…

**double** 5 to get 10, multiply by 10 and **halve** the answer:

$5 \times 13 =$    **double** 5 to get 10, multiply by 10
double

$10 \times 13 = 130$    and **halve** the answer
halve

$65$    so the answer to $5 \times 13 = 65$

Try these in the same way:

$5 \times 11 = \boxed{\phantom{00}}$    $5 \times 15 = \boxed{\phantom{00}}$    $17 \times 5 = \boxed{\phantom{00}}$    $23 \times 5 = \boxed{\phantom{00}}$

## Solve it

How much would it cost to talk on these mobile phones for 5 minutes?

**Mobility**
Cheap rate of only 26p a minute

**Cheap talk**
Only 29p a minute

**Purple**
Call for only 24p a minute

**Easy Chat**
36p a minute day and night

**Cell call**
Price: 55p per minute

**On the move**
Low charges!! 47p a minute

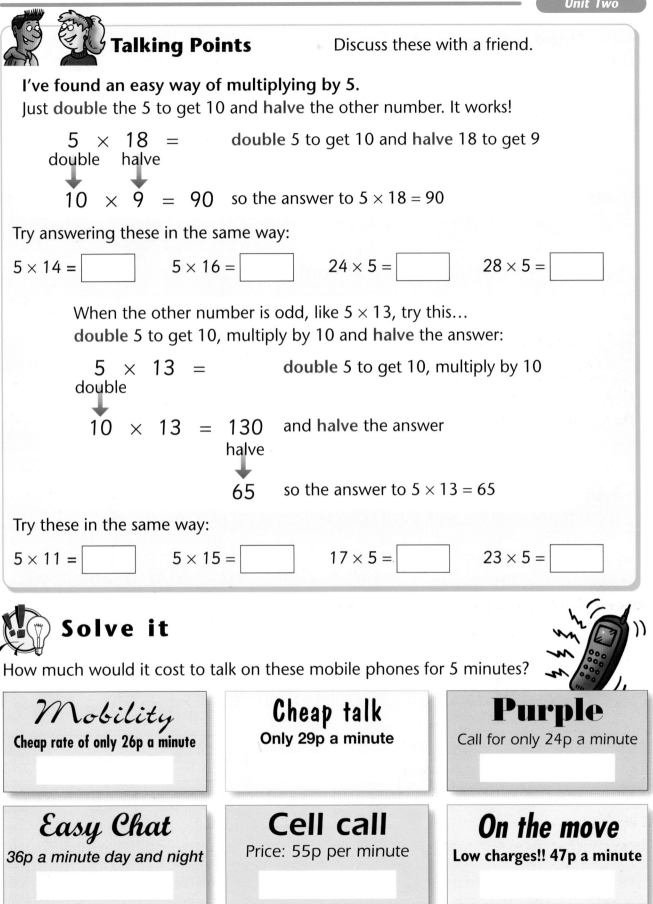

 **Let's investigate**

How fast does your heart beat?
How many times does it beat :

in a minute? .................................................................

in an hour? .................................................................

in a day? .................................................................

in a year? .................................................................

How many times has it beaten in your lifetime? .........................

**Game on**

Play this game with a friend.
You will need counters in two colours
or a coloured pencil each and three dice.

| 16 | 24 | 17 |
| 41 | 28 | |
| 45 | 26 | 15 |

1   Choose a number from the poster.
2   Roll the dice and multiply the dice number by your chosen number.
3   If the answer is in the grid, put a counter on it or colour it in.

The winner is the first to
get four in a line. The line
can be horizontal, vertical
or diagonal.

| 80 | 225 | 90 | 205 | 26 | 51 |
|-----|-----|-----|-----|-----|-----|
| 17 | 102 | 82 | 130 | 112 | 68 |
| 135 | 48 | 85 | 120 | 72 | 64 |
| 32 | 56 | 123 | 84 | 168 | 180 |
| 24 | 144 | 104 | 42 | 70 | 140 |
| 45 | 34 | 72 | 52 | 28 | 156 |

**Facts to learn:** Remember to learn division facts ready for Unit Three!

# UNIT THREE  Division

In this unit you will learn:

&#9733;  ways to help you divide in your head and on paper
&#9733;  to divide by 10 and 100
&#9733;  whether to round up or down after a division question
&#9733;  to solve real-life problems.

## 3–4 Warm up – workout!

Test yourself on the division facts from Unit Two:

| | |
|---|---|
| 12 ÷ 4 = .......... | 35 ÷ 5 = .......... |
| 72 ÷ 8 = .......... | 45 ÷ 9 = .......... |
| 81 ÷ 9 = .......... | 48 ÷ 6 = .......... |
| 42 ÷ 7 = .......... | 63 ÷ 7 = .......... |
| 27 ÷ 9 = .......... | 24 ÷ 6 = .......... |

| | |
|---|---|
| 27 ÷ 3 = .......... | 42 ÷ 6 = .......... |
| 36 ÷ 6 = .......... | 63 ÷ 9 = .......... |
| 72 ÷ 9 = .......... | 24 ÷ 4 = .......... |
| 48 ÷ 8 = .......... | 45 ÷ 5 = .......... |
| 12 ÷ 3 = .......... | 35 ÷ 7 = .......... |

## Remember

Division is the '**inverse**' of mutiplication (and so multiplication is the **inverse** of division). This means that they 'undo' each other, like this:

$$30 \div 5 = 6 \quad \text{and so} \quad 5 \times 6 = 30$$

Watch out! – It **does** matter which way round the numbers in a division fact are, the answers are not the same.

$$\boxed{24} \div \boxed{6} = 4 \qquad \boxed{6} \div \boxed{24} = 0.25!$$

## Activity

Choose three of the division statements above and write a sentence for each of them using the phrases '**shared between**', '**groups of**', and '**divided by**' like this: 'There are 6 **groups** of 4 in 24'.

_____

_____

_____

# Word work

Do you know what all these words mean? Tick those you are sure you know.

| divide   lots of   share   groups of |
| --- |
| divided by   shared between   factor |
| double   halve   remainder |
| inverse   multiple |

# Skills builder

Look at what happens when we divide by **10** and **100**. Let's pick a number to divide, like **4500**.

÷ **10**    digits move one place to the right

÷ **100**   digits move two places to the right

| Th | H | T | U |
| --- | --- | --- | --- |
| 4 | 5 | 0 | 0 |
|   | 4 | 5 | 0 |
|   |   | 4 | 5 |

**True or False?**

Who is telling the truth? Tick the correct statement in each pair.

I think …

I think …

| | |
| --- | --- |
| 4600 shared between 10 is 46 | 4600 shared between 10 is 460 |
| 360 ÷ 10 = 36 | 360 ÷ 10 = 3600 |
| 2700 divided by 100 is 270 | 2700 divided by 100 is 27 |
| 65000 ÷ 100 = 65 | 65000 ÷ 100 = 650 |
| There are 97 groups of 100 in 9700 | There are 97 groups of 100 in 97000 |

**Top tip!** *If a number divides equally into another number, the first number is a factor of the second number, so 3 is a factor of 12.*

Write 5 factors of 16

.......... .......... ..........

.......... ..........

Write 8 factors of 24

.......... .......... .......... ..........

.......... .......... .......... ..........

**Top tip!** *If a number divides equally into another number, the second number is a multiple of the first, so 12 is a multiple of 3.*

Write 5 multiples of 4

.......... .......... ..........

.......... ..........

Write 5 multiples of 6

.......... .......... ..........

.......... ..........

# Game on

Play this game with a friend. You will need a set of 0–9 digit cards.

1 Take it in turns to pick 3 cards.
2 Arrange them to make a 2-digit and a 1-digit number.
3 Divide the 2-digit number by the 1-digit number.
4 Score a point if the answer is a whole number with no remainder, like 12 ÷ 3.

$$\boxed{4}\ \boxed{5}\ \div\ \boxed{9}$$

Variation: Score a point for every way you can arrange the 3 cards to give a whole number answer when you divide e.g. 12 ÷ 3, 21 ÷ 3, 32 ÷ 1, 23 ÷ 1.

## Facts to learn for Unit Four

Another way of saying a division fact is by using fractions, like this:

$12 \div 3 = 4$ and $\frac{1}{3}$ of 12 is 4

These division facts have been written using fractions. Learn them for the next unit.

$\frac{1}{2}$ of 16 = 8     $\frac{1}{4}$ of 20 = 5     $\frac{1}{5}$ of 35 = 7     $\frac{1}{10}$ of 70 = 7     $\frac{1}{2}$ of 18 = 9

$\frac{1}{8}$ of 24 = 3     $\frac{1}{3}$ of 21 = 7     $\frac{1}{6}$ of 36 = 6     $\frac{1}{9}$ of 63 = 7     $\frac{1}{7}$ of 56 = 8

# Skills builder

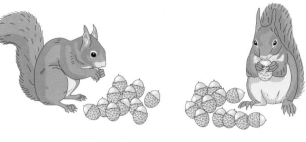

Two squirrels are dividing their acorns
into five piles to hide away for winter.
They do it like this:

'We've got 72 acorns. Let's see,
we can start with 10 in each pile.
That's 50 gone and 22 left.
We can put another 4 in each pile.
That makes 14 in each pile with 2 left over.'

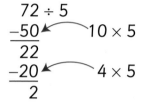

$$72 \div 5$$
$$-50 \quad 10 \times 5$$
$$\overline{\phantom{-}22}$$
$$-20 \quad 4 \times 5$$
$$\overline{\phantom{-}2}$$

Answer: **14 remainder 2**

Try these:

| | | |
|---|---|---|
| $47 \div 4$ | $56 \div 5$ | $75 \div 6$ |
| $78 \div 7$ | $83 \div 8$ | $102 \div 8$ |

## Talking Points

Sometimes remainders don't make sense! Look at this question:

19 children are going on a trip.
Each car takes 4 children.
How many cars are needed?

$19 \div 4 = 4$ remainder 3
What does this mean? Can all the children go?
We need **5** cars to get all the children there.
So the answer is 5 cars!

# Solve it

## D.I.Y City

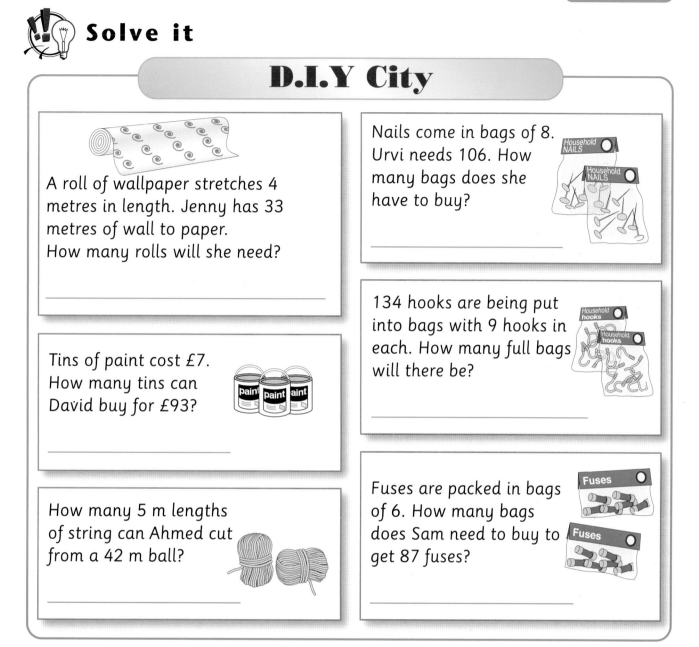

A roll of wallpaper stretches 4 metres in length. Jenny has 33 metres of wall to paper. How many rolls will she need?

_____

Tins of paint cost £7. How many tins can David buy for £93?

_____

How many 5 m lengths of string can Ahmed cut from a 42 m ball?

_____

Nails come in bags of 8. Urvi needs 106. How many bags does she have to buy?

_____

134 hooks are being put into bags with 9 hooks in each. How many full bags will there be?

_____

Fuses are packed in bags of 6. How many bags does Sam need to buy to get 87 fuses?

_____

## Let's investigate

Find out how you can tell if a number can be divided by another number without leaving a remainder.

**2** All even numbers are exactly divisible by **2**, like 34, 48 or 346.

**4** An even number that can be halved to leave another even number is exactly divisible by **4**, like 24, 40 and 248.

What can you say about numbers that are exactly divisible by **5** and by **10**? Find out about other numbers.

# ❓ Question cracker

## Show your working

Calculate 112 ÷ 9

## Show your working

A car park has spaces for 132 cars on six floors.
How many spaces are on each floor?

## Answer these questions.

Dinesh is packing eggs into boxes of 6. He has 117 eggs to pack.

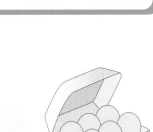

How many boxes will he need?

How many boxes will be full?

Carol has 107 photos. Each page in her album holds 8 photos.

How many pages will she need?

How many pages will be full?

**Facts to learn:** Remember to learn fraction facts on page 15!

# UNIT FOUR Fractions and Percentages

In this unit you will learn:

&#9733;  how fractions and percentages work
&#9733;  how to change a fraction to its lowest terms
&#9733;  how to order mixed numbers
&#9733;  how to solve problems involving fractions and percentages.

## Warm up – workout!

Test yourself on the division facts from Unit Three:

$\frac{1}{2}$ of 16 = ........    $\frac{1}{3}$ of 21 = ........    $\frac{1}{10}$ of 70 = ........    $\frac{1}{7}$ of 56 = ........    $\frac{1}{2}$ of 18 = ........

$\frac{1}{8}$ of 24 = ........    $\frac{1}{5}$ of 35 = ........    $\frac{1}{6}$ of 36 = ........    $\frac{1}{9}$ of 63 = ........    $\frac{1}{4}$ of 20 = ........

## Word work

Do you know what all these words mean?
Discuss each of them with a partner.
Circle those you are sure you know.

Fill in the missing word from each
sentence with one of these words:

> fraction    numerator
> mixed number    denominator
> equivalent    percentage
> per cent    hundredth

One half is ............................................. to two quarters.

The ............................................. of $\frac{3}{4}$ is 4.

$2\frac{1}{4}$ is known as a ............................................. .

Three quarters, when written as a ............................................. , is 75%

5 is the ............................................. of $\frac{5}{8}$ .

**True or false?**  Henry the Eighth invented fractions.

A fraction is when something is split into equal parts, like a group of children, a price or a bar of chocolate.

2/5 of children asked watched the afternoon film on Boxing Day

½ price tickets!

1/3 off cost of all items!

MAN ATE 3/4 OF A BAR OF CHOCOLATE IN 5 MINUTES!

## Skills builder

The number on the bottom of the fraction (the denominator) tells us how many equal parts something has been split into. The number on the top of the fraction (the numerator) tells us how many of these parts we are looking at.

$\frac{3}{4}$ numerator / denominator

$\frac{3}{4}$ of a bar of chocolate has been split into 4 equal parts

and we are looking at 3 of them.

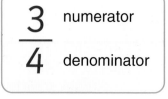

Here are some fractions that are equivalent – they mean the same thing! Can you see why?

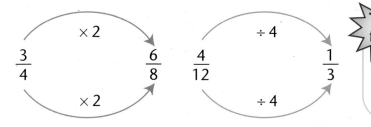

Look at the numbers in the pairs of equivalent fractions.

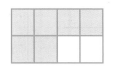

$\frac{3}{4}$ ×2 $\frac{6}{8}$ ×2

$\frac{4}{12}$ ÷4 $\frac{1}{3}$ ÷4

**Top tip!** *As long as you multiply or divide both the numerator and the denominator by the same number the fraction will be equivalent.*

Tick the all fractions that are equivalent to the fraction in the star.

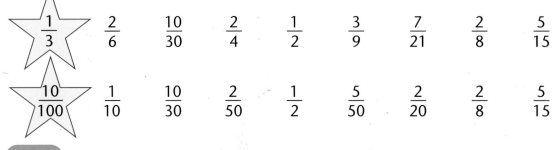

$\frac{1}{3}$  $\frac{2}{6}$  $\frac{10}{30}$  $\frac{2}{4}$  $\frac{1}{2}$  $\frac{3}{9}$  $\frac{7}{21}$  $\frac{2}{8}$  $\frac{5}{15}$

$\frac{10}{100}$  $\frac{1}{10}$  $\frac{10}{30}$  $\frac{2}{50}$  $\frac{1}{2}$  $\frac{5}{50}$  $\frac{2}{20}$  $\frac{2}{8}$  $\frac{5}{15}$

## Talking Points

Sometimes it's easier to use the *simplest fraction* when solving problems.

$$\frac{6}{24} \qquad \frac{22}{88} \qquad \frac{36}{144} \qquad \frac{1}{4} \qquad \frac{14}{56} \qquad \frac{4}{16} \cdot \qquad \frac{3}{12} \qquad \frac{100}{400}$$

Which do you think is the simplest fraction to work with? Why?
Ask a partner if they agree.

## Skills builder

To change a fraction to its simplest form (sometimes called *lowest terms*), first find a number that will divide exactly into both the numerator and denominator. Then divide both by this number.

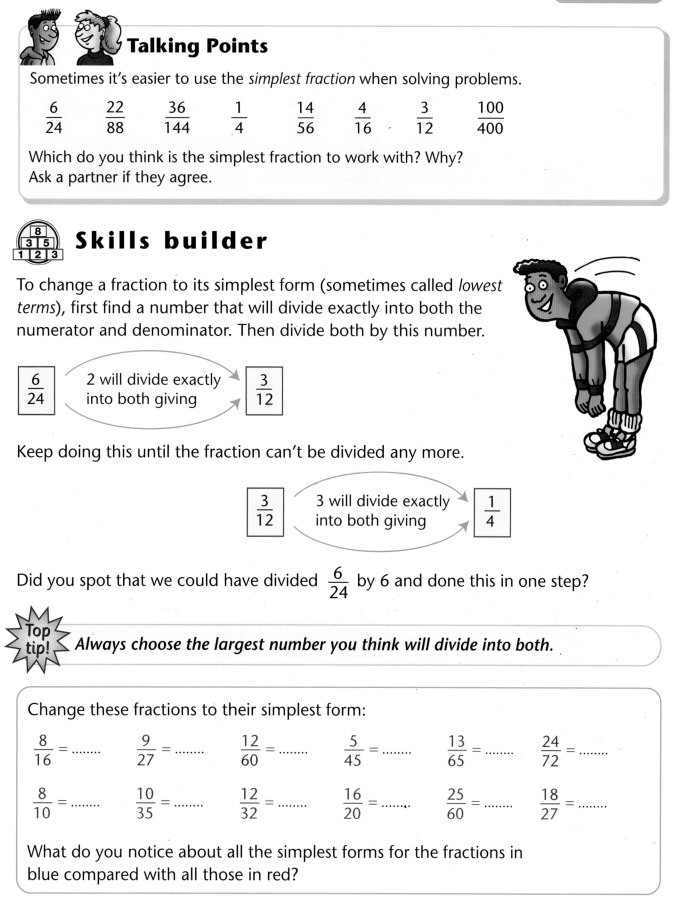

$$\boxed{\frac{6}{24}}$$  2 will divide exactly into both giving  $$\boxed{\frac{3}{12}}$$

Keep doing this until the fraction can't be divided any more.

$$\boxed{\frac{3}{12}}$$  3 will divide exactly into both giving  $$\boxed{\frac{1}{4}}$$

Did you spot that we could have divided $\frac{6}{24}$ by 6 and done this in one step?

**Top tip!** *Always choose the largest number you think will divide into both.*

Change these fractions to their simplest form:

$$\frac{8}{16} = \text{.......} \qquad \frac{9}{27} = \text{.......} \qquad \frac{12}{60} = \text{.......} \qquad \frac{5}{45} = \text{.......} \qquad \frac{13}{65} = \text{.......} \qquad \frac{24}{72} = \text{.......}$$

$$\frac{8}{10} = \text{.......} \qquad \frac{10}{35} = \text{.......} \qquad \frac{12}{32} = \text{.......} \qquad \frac{16}{20} = \text{.......} \qquad \frac{25}{60} = \text{.......} \qquad \frac{18}{27} = \text{.......}$$

What do you notice about all the simplest forms for the fractions in blue compared with all those in red?

# Skills builder

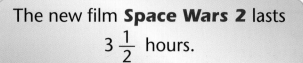

The new film **Space Wars 2** lasts $3\frac{1}{2}$ hours.

$3\frac{1}{2}$ is a **mixed number** as it has a whole number (three) and a fraction (a half).

Here are the lengths of some films in hours:

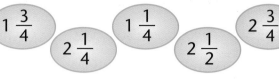

$1\frac{3}{4}$  $2\frac{1}{4}$  $1\frac{1}{4}$  $2\frac{1}{2}$  $2\frac{3}{4}$

We can put these mixed numbers in order like this:

1 Compare the whole numbers first.
2 If the whole numbers are the same, compare the fractions.

Write the mixed numbers in order, smallest first.

........................................................................................................

# Question cracker

Arrange these fractions in order from largest to smallest:

$5\frac{1}{2}$        $5\frac{3}{5}$        $4\frac{4}{5}$        $5\frac{1}{5}$        $5\frac{4}{5}$

Put these fractions in order and mark them on the number line:

$2\frac{1}{2}$        $1\frac{3}{4}$        $2\frac{1}{4}$        $\frac{3}{4}$        $2\frac{3}{4}$

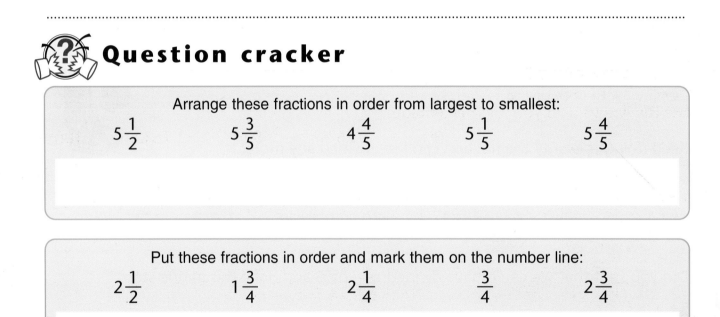

# Game on

A game for 2, 3 or 4 players. Write 12 mixed numbers between 1 and 4 on cards. Shuffle the cards and share them out, but don't look at them. Count to three and then each player turns over their top card. The player whose card is the largest mixed number keeps all the cards. The winner is the player who ends up with all the cards.

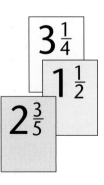

$3\frac{1}{4}$  $1\frac{1}{2}$  $2\frac{3}{5}$

# Skills builder

**30% off!**

**10% sale** **5% increase**

We use the symbol **%** to show percentages.
**Per cent** means 'out of every hundred'.

Thirty per cent means 30 out of 100.

$$30\% = \frac{30}{100}$$

Fractions and percentages are closely related. A percentage is just a fraction with a **denominator** of 100.

Write these percentages as fractions, and, where you can, change the fractions to their simplest form.

50% = ............................    25% = ............................    10% = ............................

75% = ............................    5% = ............................    12% = ............................

# Solve it

Use the line to help you find percentages.

| 0% | 25% | 50% | 75% | 100% |
|----|-----|-----|-----|------|
| 0 | $\frac{1}{4}$ | $\frac{1}{2}$ | $\frac{3}{4}$ | 1 |

To find 50% of something, find $\frac{1}{2}$

To find 25% find $\frac{1}{4}$

To find 75% find $\frac{3}{4}$

Find the new prices:

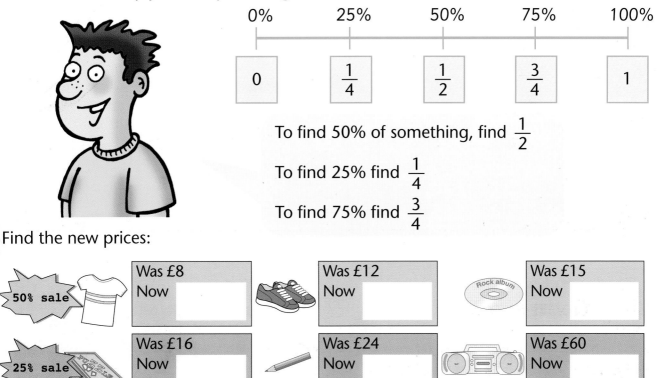

50% sale — Was £8 Now

Was £12 Now

Was £15 Now

25% sale — Was £16 Now

Was £24 Now

Was £60 Now

75% sale — Was £40 Now

Was £60 Now

Was £200 Now

 ## Let's investigate

One of the best ways to work out other percentages of numbers is to find **10%** first, because you can:     double it to find 20%,
halve it to find 5% and so on.

How can you find **10%** of a number?
How could you then find 40%, 30%? What about 80%?
Choose some multiples of 10, like 50, 90 or 150. Find 10% of each of them and then find as many other percentages of these numbers as you can.

...................................................................................................................................................................
...................................................................................................................................................................
...................................................................................................................................................................
...................................................................................................................................................................

## Solve it

Work with a partner to decide which you would prefer:

> 75% of £40     or     25% of £80

> 20% of £70     or     60% of £20

> 5% of £100     or     30% of £20

> 90% of £50     or     10% of £400

> 35% of £60     or     70% of £90

### Things to know for Unit Five

These are some multiplication and division facts like those you met in earlier units.
Make sure you remember how to do them before starting Unit Five.

| | | |
|---|---|---|
| $40 \times 10 = 400$ | $95 \times 10 = 950$ | $10 \times 200 = 2000$ |
| $100 \times 50 = 5000$ | $63 \times 100 = 6300$ | $100 \times 99 = 9900$ |
| $200 \div 10 = 20$ | $450 \div 10 = 45$ | $730 \div 10 = 73$ |
| $300 \div 100 = 3$ | $6000 \div 100 = 60$ | $8700 \div 100 = 87$ |

# UNIT FIVE  Place Value and Decimals

In this unit you will learn:

- ★ how to write large numbers in figures and words
- ★ how to round large numbers
- ★ how to put large numbers in order of size
- ★ about decimals, including how to add them.

## Warm up – workout!

*Cover the page opposite!*

Test yourself on the facts from Unit Four:

$200 \div 10 =$ ............     $100 \times 99 =$ ............     $10 \times 200 =$ ............

$100 \times 50 =$ ............     $300 \div 100 =$ ............     $6000 \div 100 =$ ............

$95 \times 10 =$ ............     $40 \times 10 =$ ............     $450 \div 10 =$ ............

$730 \div 10 =$ ............     $63 \times 100 =$ ............     $8700 \div 100 =$ ............

## Remember!

When we **multiply** by 10 and 100 the digits move to the **left**

so $62 \times 10$ becomes 620
so $62 \times 100$ becomes 6200

| Th | H | T | U |
|----|---|---|---|
|    |   | 6 | 2 |
|    | 6 | 2 | 0 |
| 6  | 2 | 0 | 0 |

When we **divide** by 10 and 100 the digits move to the **right**

so $3700 \div 10$ becomes 370
so $3700 \div 100$ becomes 37

| Th | H | T | U |
|----|---|---|---|
| 3  | 7 | 0 | 0 |
|    | 3 | 7 | 0 |
|    |   | 3 | 7 |

## Let's investigate

How many different numbers can you make using these 3 digits?
34, 743,  ...................................................................................................................

.............................................................................................................................................

Can you write them in order, smallest first?

.............................................................................................................................................

Explore how many you can make using 4 digits.

# Word work

digit    numeral    place value    round down
less than    decimal    approximate    decimal point
round up    decimal place    greater than

Here's a challenge for you. Write sentences about these numbers using some of the words above.

3 ....................................................................................................................

67 ....................................................................................................................

106 ....................................................................................................................

5.9 ....................................................................................................................

7.02 ....................................................................................................................

# Skills builder

How good are you at writing large numbers in figures and words?

It's always a good idea to use column headings, separating the number of thousands from the hundreds, tens and units. Sometimes we use a space to do this: **635 294**

| Hundred thousands | Ten thousands | Thousands | Hundreds | Tens | Units |
|---|---|---|---|---|---|
| 6 | 3 | 5 | 2 | 9 | 4 |

Six hundred and thirty five thousand two hundred and ninety four

| Write these numbers in words: | 428 916 |
|---|---|
| | 281 532 |
| | 506 291 |

## Solve it    Write the numbers in the reports in words

> ### The Daily News    **August 1st 2000**
> 74 251 people filled Wembley last night to see England play the

...........................................................................................................

> ### The Sunday Reporter    **July 30th 2000**
> Mrs Jones of Stalybridge won £254 071 on the lottery yesterday.
> She is going on a holiday but will give most of it to her children.

...........................................................................................................

> ## THE WEEKLY MAIL    **AUGUST 4 2000**
> The Spice Girls played to a full house of 12 009 in Birmingham last night. It was

...........................................................................................................

**Quiz Show!**  Write these numbers as numerals and check your answers with a partner.

> Mount Everest is twenty nine thousand and thirty feet high.

> The Caspian Sea has an area of three hundred and seventy thousand and eighty square kilometres.

> The area of Iceland is one hundred and three thousand and ten square kilometres.

## Game on

This is a game for two or more players. You will need 0–9 digit cards.

1  Turn over five cards each and make the largest number you can.
2  Compare the numbers and read your own aloud.
3  Score a point for the largest number if you have read it correctly.

The winner is the first player to score 11 points.

# Skills builder

Look at this football attendance:

Man. United v Spurs

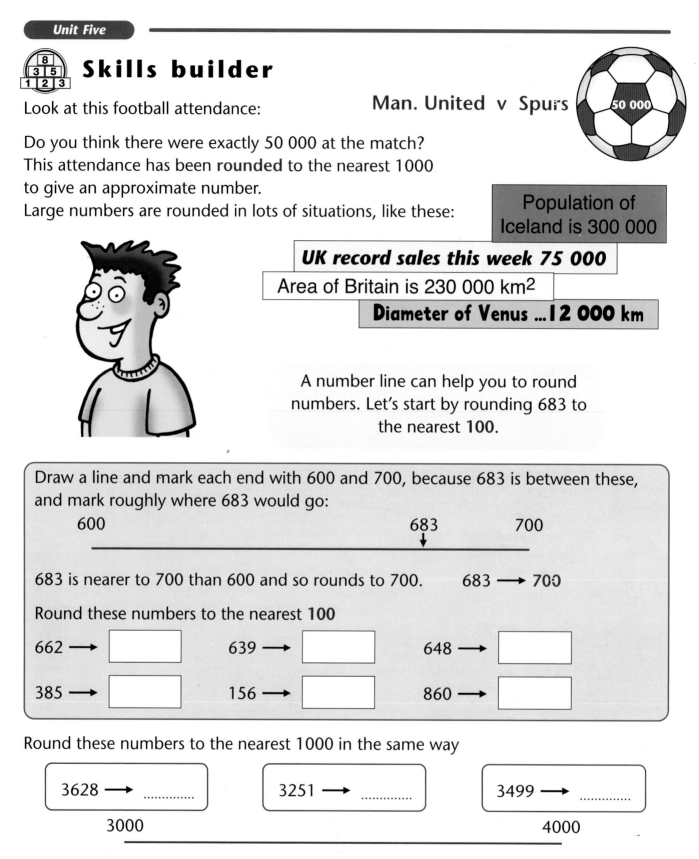

50 000

Do you think there were exactly 50 000 at the match?
This attendance has been **rounded** to the nearest 1000
to give an approximate number.
Large numbers are rounded in lots of situations, like these:

Population of Iceland is 300 000

UK record sales this week 75 000

Area of Britain is 230 000 km²

Diameter of Venus ...12 000 km

A number line can help you to round
numbers. Let's start by rounding 683 to
the nearest **100**.

Draw a line and mark each end with 600 and 700, because 683 is between these,
and mark roughly where 683 would go:

600                                                683          700

683 is nearer to 700 than 600 and so rounds to 700.      683 ⟶ 700

Round these numbers to the nearest **100**

662 ⟶ [　　]          639 ⟶ [　　]          648 ⟶ [　　]

385 ⟶ [　　]          156 ⟶ [　　]          860 ⟶ [　　]

Round these numbers to the nearest 1000 in the same way

3628 ⟶ ...........          3251 ⟶ ...........          3499 ⟶ ...........

3000                                                          4000

How many people do you think might have been at the Man. United v Spurs match?
Why do you think this?

...................................................................................................

### Talking Points

Sometimes the number we have to round is exactly in the middle, like these:

| 500 | 550 | 600 | 3000 | 3500 | 4000 |

What do we do when this happens? How could we round 6500 to the nearest 1000?

### Question cracker

These results are all decimal numbers. We use decimals when the unit we are using, like metres or seconds, is too large and must be split into smaller parts.

**news *** Olympic Games winning times and distances *** news**

| 100 metres | 9.78 secs | 400 metres | 44.21 secs |
| Long jump | 8.43 m | Weightlifting | 137.07 kg |

**9.78** secs means **9** whole seconds, **7** tenths of a second and **8** hundredths of a second.
We can show this using column headings:

```
U . t h
9 . 7 8
```

What is the red digit worth in each of these numbers?

8.43 ...........................     44.21 ...........................     137.07 ...........................

20.82 ...........................     156.17 ...........................     400.08 ...........................

Compare the box below with the one on the page 25.
Look at the column headings and see the effect of multiplying and dividing by 10 and 100.

### Facts

When we **multiply** by 10 and 100 the digits move to the **left**

so 0.57 × 10 becomes 5.7
so 0.57 × 100 becomes 57

| T | U | . | t | h |
|---|---|---|---|---|
|   |   | . | 5 | 7 |
|   | 5 | . | 7 | 0 |
| 5 | 7 | . | 0 | 0 |

When we **divide** by 10 and 100 the digits move to the **right**

so 24 ÷ 10 becomes 2.4
so 24 ÷ 100 becomes 0.24

| T | U | . | t | h |
|---|---|---|---|---|
| 2 | 4 | . | 0 | 0 |
|   | 2 | . | 4 | 0 |
|   |   | . | 2 | 4 |

 **Let's investigate**

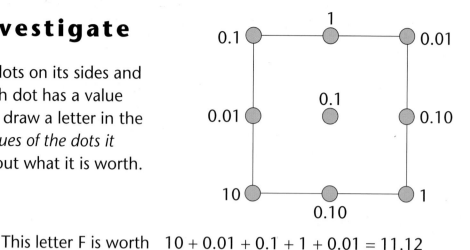

This square has eight dots on its sides and one in the middle. Each dot has a value shown next to it. If we draw a letter in the square and *add the values of the dots it touches*, we can work out what it is worth.

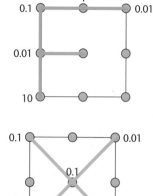

This letter F is worth   $10 + 0.01 + 0.1 + 1 + 0.01 = 11.12$

Work out the values of these letters.

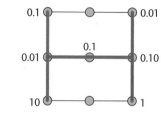 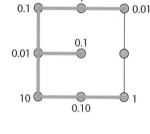 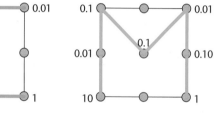

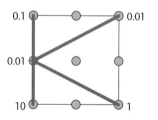 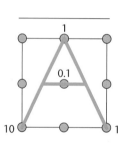 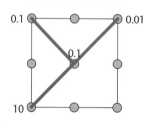 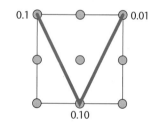

Which letter has the highest value? ............... lowest value? ...............

Can you find other letters that have higher or lower values than these?

How much is your name worth? ........................................

**Things to know for Unit Five**

| Learn the multiples | of | 7 | 7, 14, 21, 28, 35, 42, 49, 56, 63, 70 ... |
| --- | --- | --- | --- |
| | of | 8 | 8, 16, 24, 32, 40, 48, 56, 64, 72, 80 ... |
| | of | 9 | 9, 18, 27, 36, 45, 54, 63, 72, 81, 90 ... |

# UNIT SIX  Number Patterns

In this unit you will learn:

★ how to explore and continue number patterns
★ how to describe the patterns in a sequence
★ about square numbers, multiples and factors
★ to use a simple formula.

## Warm up – workout!

*Cover the page opposite!*

Test yourself on the multiples from Unit Five:

Circle the multiples of 7 (7) . Draw squares around multiples of 8 [8] .
Draw triangles around multiples of 9 /9\ .
Some numbers may need two shapes!

21      64      35      81      63      54      56

45      49      42      72      48      36

## Word work

| multiple   factor   square number   consecutive   increases by   decreases by |
| difference   negative   number pattern   sequence   formula   positive |

Who is telling the truth about this number pattern? (Tick the correct sentences.)

27   24   21   18   15   12   9 ...

*These numbers are multiples of 3.*

*Three is a factor of all these numbers.*

*The numbers in this sequence are negative numbers.*

*The difference between 27 and 24 is 3.*

*The numbers in this sequence increase by 3 each time.*

*These numbers are positive numbers.*

*The numbers in this pattern decrease by 3 each time.*

## Skills builder

Count the number of small squares in each of these pictures.
Write underneath how many there are.

_____          _____          _____          _____

Do you know what these numbers are called? They are **square numbers** because we can draw them as squares.

Each square number is the result of multiplying a number by itself:
$1 \times 1$          $2 \times 2$          $3 \times 3$          $4 \times 4$          $5 \times 5$

We use the symbol $^2$ to mean '**squared**', so
$\qquad 2^2$ means $2 \times 2$.      We say $2^2$ as '**two squared**'.
$\qquad 3^2$ means $3 \times 3$, and so on.

Look at the list of square numbers below. Write the next three in the sequence.

$\qquad 1^2 \qquad 2^2 \qquad 3^2 \qquad 4^2 \qquad 5^2 \qquad 6^2 \qquad$ ............ ............

$\qquad 1 \qquad\quad 4 \qquad\quad 19 \qquad\quad 16 \qquad\quad 25 \qquad$ ............ ............ ............

## Let's investigate

How did you work them out? You can use the line of difference, like this:

difference    3          5          7          9          ............          ............

1          4          9          16          25          ............

Carry on the sequence using the differences until you reach 144 (or more!).

.........................................................................................................................................................

.........................................................................................................................................................

.........................................................................................................................................................

# Skills builder

To work out how any sequence continues, look at consecutive numbers in it and find the difference between them. In some sequences the difference is the same.

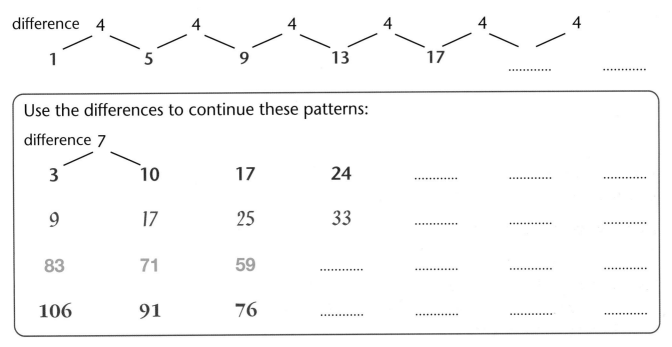

difference    4         4         4         4         4         4

1         5         9         13        17        ............    ............

Use the differences to continue these patterns:

difference 7

| 3 | 10 | 17 | 24 | ............ | ............ | ............ |
| 9 | 17 | 25 | 33 | ............ | ............ | ............ |
| 83 | 71 | 59 | ............ | ............ | ............ | ............ |
| 106 | 91 | 76 | ............ | ............ | ............ | ............ |

Can you describe to a friend how these sequences work?
Use words like **increasing, decreasing, difference**.

  **Talking Points**

Who has given the best answer to this question?

> 1    4    7    10    13    ...
> **What is the next number in the sequence?**
> **Explain how you worked this out.**

*I saw the pattern and knew it was 16.*

*The numbers in the pattern are increasing by 3 each time. I added 3 to 13 to make 16 to get the next number.*

*16. I just guessed.*

# Solve it

Can you see number patterns in these situations?

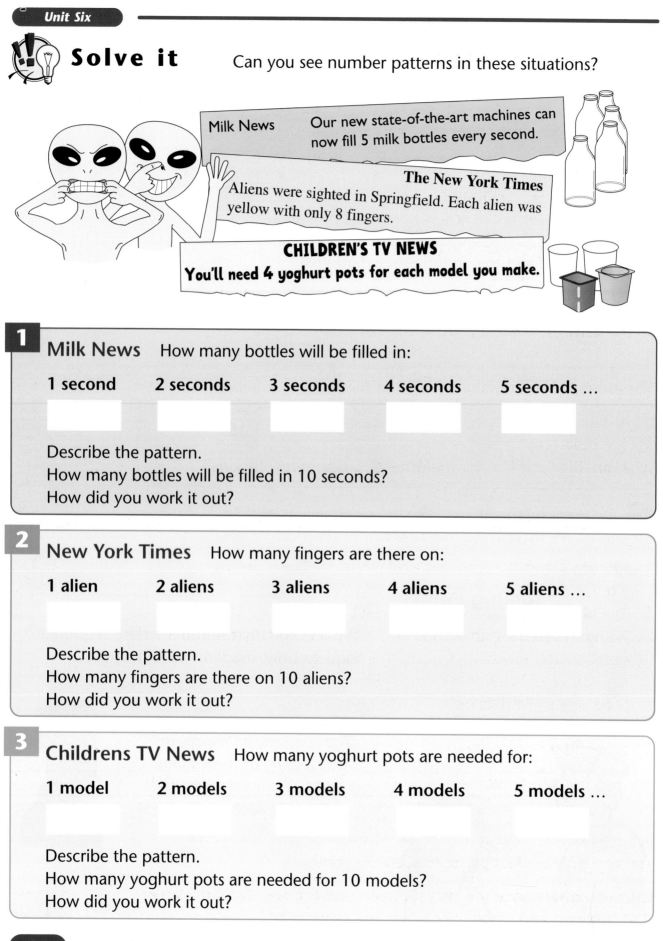

Milk News    Our new state-of-the-art machines can now fill 5 milk bottles every second.

**The New York Times**
Aliens were sighted in Springfield. Each alien was yellow with only 8 fingers.

**CHILDREN'S TV NEWS**
You'll need 4 yoghurt pots for each model you make.

## 1 Milk News    How many bottles will be filled in:

| 1 second | 2 seconds | 3 seconds | 4 seconds | 5 seconds … |
|---|---|---|---|---|
|  |  |  |  |  |

Describe the pattern.
How many bottles will be filled in 10 seconds?
How did you work it out?

## 2 New York Times    How many fingers are there on:

| 1 alien | 2 aliens | 3 aliens | 4 aliens | 5 aliens … |
|---|---|---|---|---|
|  |  |  |  |  |

Describe the pattern.
How many fingers are there on 10 aliens?
How did you work it out?

## 3 Childrens TV News    How many yoghurt pots are needed for:

| 1 model | 2 models | 3 models | 4 models | 5 models … |
|---|---|---|---|---|
|  |  |  |  |  |

Describe the pattern.
How many yoghurt pots are needed for 10 models?
How did you work it out?

# Skills builder

Look at the Milk News opposite. The machines fill 5 bottles each second. How many can be filled in 100 or 500 seconds? Here's a good way of finding out.

Did you spot that the number of bottles filled is always five times the number of seconds?

We say the number of bottles filled is: $5 \times n$

$n$ is a code that stands for the number of seconds.
All we have to do is swap $n$ for the number of seconds in the question.

So the number of bottles filled in 100 seconds is $5 \times n$
$5 \times 100 = 500$

The number of bottles filled in 500 seconds is $5 \times n$
$5 \times 500 = 2500$

$5 \times n$ is called the **formula**.
What are the **formulas** for the other two newspaper reports?

# Game on

Play this with a friend. Take turns to use the calculator.

1   Choose a start number and a rule from the boxes below
    e.g.  36 add 11
2   The player with the calculator presses 36 + + 11 =
3   Without looking at the calculator, begin and continue to call out the
    numbers in the sequence from the start number, using the rule,
    e.g.  36 (add 11) 47    58    69    80    91    102
4   Stop when 100 is passed.
5   The player with the calculator keeps pressing the = key to check the
    other player's numbers.

| start numbers: |
| :---: |
| 1    11    19    27    36    41 |

| rules: |
| :---: |
| add 5    add 11    add 13    add 21 |

Score a point for saying the sequence correctly.
The winner is the first player to score 11 points.

Later you can change the start numbers and the rule. Try some larger
start numbers and some rules which use subtraction.

# Let's investigate

Choose a number pattern from the list below. Colour each of the numbers in the sequence on the grid. What do you notice?

1, 4, 7, 10, 13, 16

2, 5, 8, 11, 14, 17

3, 7, 11, 15, 19, 23

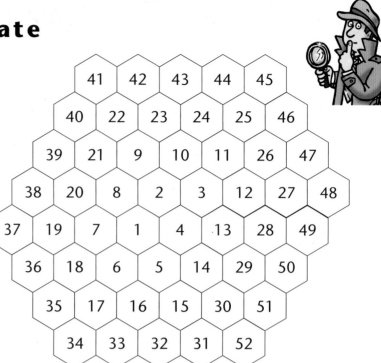

What sequence is coloured here?

.........................................................................................

Use a range of square, triangular or hexagonal paper. Write numbers in a spiral and then investigate some number sequences by colouring the numbers in.

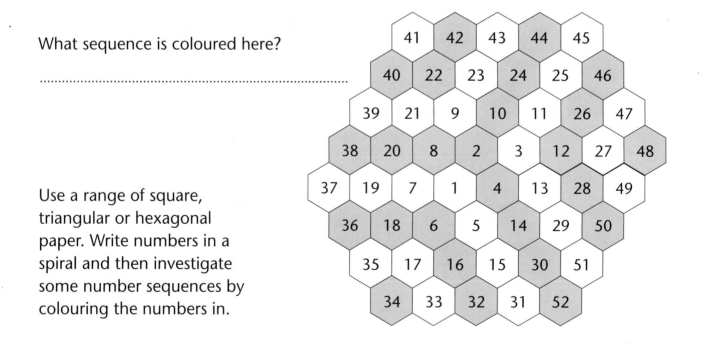

---

## Learn these 2D shape facts for Unit Seven

**Equilateral triangle** – 3 straight sides of equal length
**Isosceles triangle** – 3 straight sides, 2 that are the same length
**Scalene triangle** – 3 straight sides, all different lengths
**Quadrilateral** – 4 straight sides       **Pentagon** – 5 straight sides
**Hexagon** – 6 straight sides              **Octagon** – 8 straight sides

# UNIT SEVEN 2D Shapes, Area and Co-ordinates

In this unit you will learn:

- ★ more about 2D shapes
- ★ how to recognise parallel and perpendicular lines
- ★ how to find the area of shapes
- ★ how to use co-ordinates
- ★ about reflections and translations.

## Warm up – workout!

Name these shapes

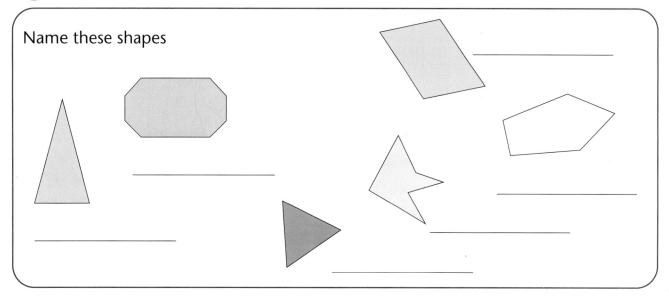

## Let's investigate

Draw this grid on squared paper and draw in the two lines. Cut along the red lines to make four identical pieces. Using all four pieces, with no overlapping, can you make each of the shapes below?

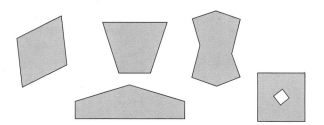

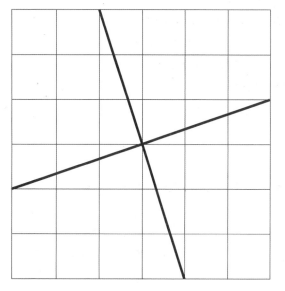

How would you describe each shape? Can you make other shapes?

# Word work

Can you name all the shapes on the grid?

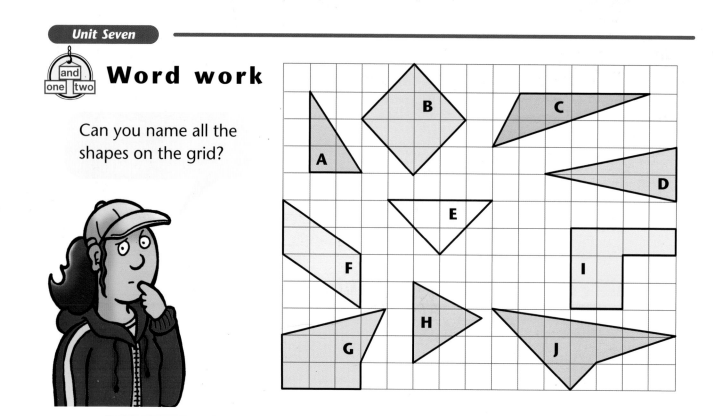

symmetry   isosceles   equilateral   scalene   quadrilateral
side   edge   polygon   area   base   vertex   regular   vertices
irregular   parallel   reflection   perpendicular

# Game on

Play this game with a friend.

Both players look at the shapes on the grid. One player chooses a shape and describes it using some of the words above. Can the other player name it correctly? If so, they have a turn to choose and describe a shape.

*It's a triangle but it's not symmetrical*

*I think it's shape A*

**True or false?**   A polygon is a dead parrot.

**Top tip!**   *Parallel lines **are** the same distance apart. They **don't** have to be the same length and they can be curved.*

**Top tip!** *Perpendicular lines* **touch or cross at** *right angles.*

 # Skills builder

*The foul was in the penalty area ...*

*We're going to work in the art area ...*

**This is the junior's play area ...**

**He delivers letters in the Reading area ...**

As well as describing shapes we can also measure their area. The word 'area' is used a lot.

Area is the amount of surface a shape covers. In flat shapes it is the space inside the lines, or boundary, of the shape. We measure area in squares, such as square centimetres ($cm^2$), square metres ($m^2$), square kilometres ($km^2$), etc.

**What is the area of the shapes opposite in squares?**

A .............................................  B .............................................  C .............................................

D .............................................  E .............................................  F .............................................

G .............................................  H .............................................  I .............................................

J .............................................

# Solve it

On centimetre-squared paper draw badges with an area of 24 square centimetres. Shade sections of each badge in 3 colours and work out the area covered by each colour

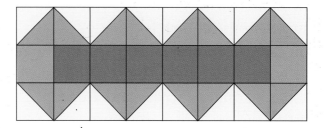

**Area of red** 6 $cm^2$     **Area of yellow** 10 $cm^2$     **Area of orange** 8 $cm^2$

Try different badge shapes, like these:

Find the area of each colour and remember – the total should be 24 $cm^2$.

# Skills builder

We can find the area of squares and rectangles by multiplying together the number of squares along each side, like this:

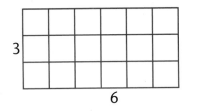

**The number of squares is 18**

**3 × 6 = 18**

**Can you see why this works?**

Write the areas inside these shapes

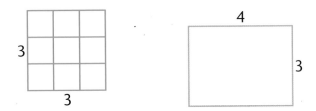

 **Question cracker**

On the grid draw a triangle with the same area as the red rectangle

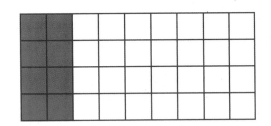

# Skills builder

*What do you mean 'it's near the middle'? Where exactly?*

Look at the map. Where is the church?
Imagine you are talking to a friend on the phone.
They have the same map as you. How can you
say where the church is **exactly?**
You can use co-ordinates. They are the numbers along
the edge of the map. The church is at (4,2). This
means **4 squares across** and **2 up**.
You always go **across**, then **up**.

Where is the pond? .............................

What is at (6,1)? .............................

Where is the tree? .............................

What is at (4, 2)? .............................

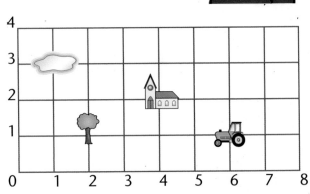

**Top tip!** *The order in which we write co-ordinates is very important. Remember it by saying 'in the house, up the stairs'*

Look at the grid on page 38. Write co-ordinates along the edges, with 0 in the bottom-left corner like on the grid opposite. Choose three shapes and write the co-ordinates for each of their vertices, like this…

shape    A    *(1,8), (3,8), (1,11)*

shape    ........

shape    ........

shape    ........

 **Game on**

Play this game with a friend. This game is set in the desert.

1   Mark six crosses on the grid where lines meet. Hide them from your friend. Each cross shows where you have buried a bottle of water.

2   Take it in turns to say a co-ordinate. If your friend has a bottle hidden there it is smashed.

Who has the last bottle left, and so who survives?
Mark all the co-ordinates you say on your own map as a check.

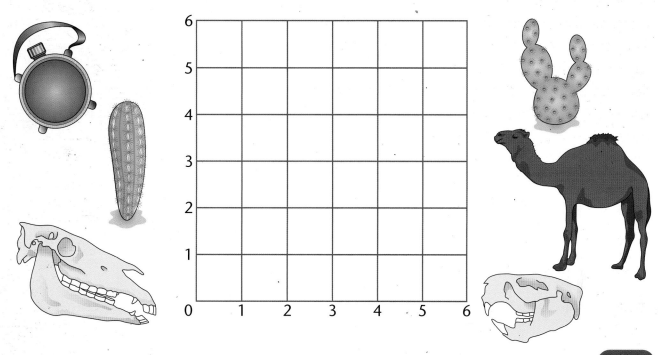

# Skills builder

As well as reflecting my cool hairstyle, we can use mirrors to reflect other things, like patterns and shapes.

Look how this shape has been reflected in the red mirror line. Pick a vertex. Its reflection is the same distance from the mirror on the opposite side. That's how reflections work.

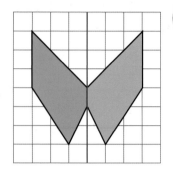

See if you can reflect these shapes:

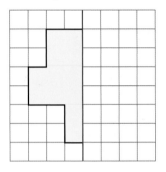

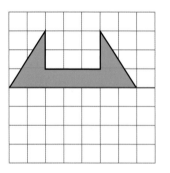

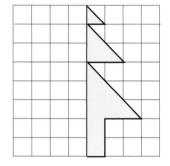

Sometimes the mirror line is diagonal, but the reflection works in the same way. Try to reflect the shapes in the two grids below.
Look at how the red and yellow dots have been reflected to help you.

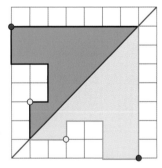

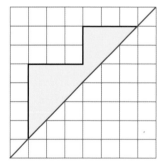

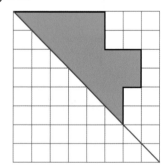

## Things to know for Unit Eight

| | | |
|---|---|---|
| $90 \times 2 = 180$ | 60 seconds = 1 minute | 30 seconds = $\frac{1}{2}$ minute |
| half of 90 = 45 | 60 minutes = 1 hour | 15 minutes = $\frac{1}{4}$ hour |
| $90 \times 3 = 270$ | 24 hours = 1 day | 7 days = 1 week |
| $90 \times 4 = 360$ | 365 days = 1 normal year | 12 months = 1 year |

# UNIT EIGHT  Angle and Time

In this unit you will learn:

★ how to name, draw and measure angles
★ to recognise angles in shapes and in the world around us
★ about recording the time in different ways
★ how to add and subtract time.

## Warm up – workout!

*Cover the page opposite!*

Test yourself on these facts from Unit Seven:

$90 \times 3 =$ ............

............ days = 1 week

............ days = 1 normal year

............ hours = 1 day

$90 \times 4 =$ ............

............ months = 1 year

............ seconds = $\frac{1}{2}$ minute

$90 \times 2 =$ ............

............ seconds = 1 minute

............ minutes = 1 hour

15 minutes = ............ hour

half of 90 = ............

## Word work

| angle | obtuse | degree | digital | acute | p.m. | clockwise | right-angle |

a.m.   protractor   anti-clockwise   analogue

## Game on

Play this game with a friend. You will need a set of cards, or pieces of paper, with each of the above words written on them.

Take turns to pick a card, read the word, and ask your partner to say what it means. If they are right, they score a point. If you disagree, use a maths dictionary to check!

# Skills builder

| Ourselves | Clock hands | Wheels |
|---|---|---|
| | Door handles | Heads |
| | Windscreen wipers | Taps |

What do all the words in the boxes have in common?

When you think you know, look at the answer at the bottom of the page.

Angles are turns. An angle is the amount something has turned.
There are different types of angle. Here are three of them:

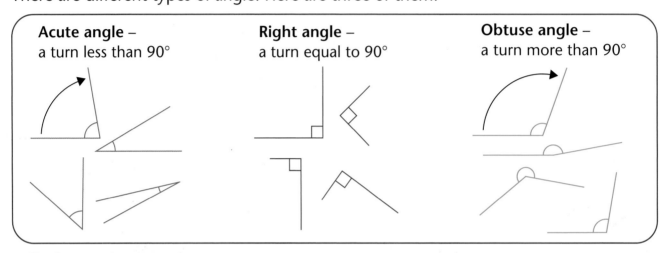

**Acute angle –** a turn less than 90°

**Right angle –** a turn equal to 90°

**Obtuse angle –** a turn more than 90°

# Question cracker

If the arrow turns clockwise to point to C, what type of angle has it turned through?

If the arrow is pointing to D and moves clockwise, what type of angle does it turn through to point to H?

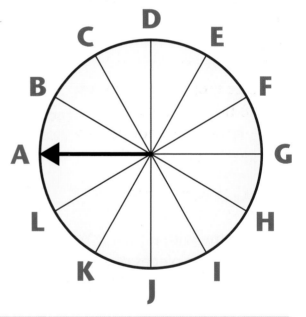

If the arrow is pointing to F, to which letter would it point if it turned through:

1 right angle?          2 right angles?          3 right angles?

4 right angles?

Answer: they're all things that turn!

# Game on

Play this game with a friend.

**1** Player 1 reads aloud one of the cards below.

**2** Player 2 scores a point for describing it correctly, like 'acute angle'.

**3** Player 2 reads a card, and so on.

**4** The winner is the first to score 7 points.

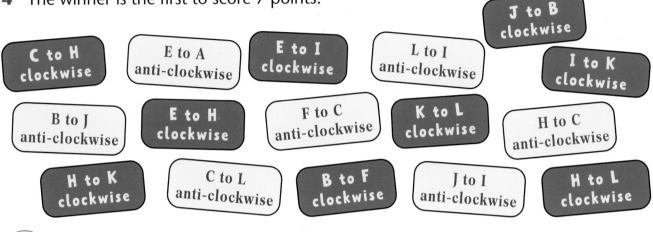

> J to B
> clockwise

> C to H
> clockwise

> E to A
> anti-clockwise

> E to I
> clockwise

> L to I
> anti-clockwise

> I to K
> clockwise

> B to J
> anti-clockwise

> E to H
> clockwise

> F to C
> anti-clockwise

> K to L
> clockwise

> H to C
> anti-clockwise

> H to K
> clockwise

> C to L
> anti-clockwise

> B to F
> clockwise

> J to I
> anti-clockwise

> H to L
> clockwise

# Skills builder

In olden days people thought that the Earth took about 360 days to go round the Sun.

This is why there are 360° in a circle. A protractor shows this, because it is split into 360 tiny divisions, called **degrees**. Each degree shows about how far the Earth turns around the Sun in one day.

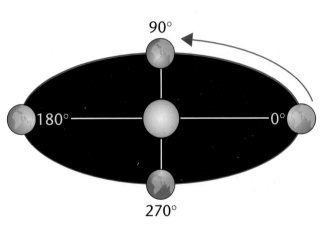

Some protractors are circular and show 360°, but others are semi-circular and show 180°, like the one below.

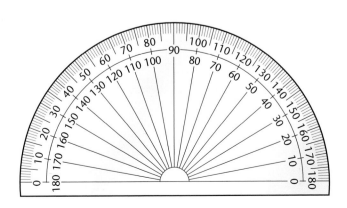

When you are drawing or measuring angles, always imagine that both lines begin on top of each other, pointing to 0°, before opening out through 10°, 20°, 30° …

Top tip!

*Don't get confused by the two sets of numbers on the protractor. Ask, 'Is the angle acute or obtuse?' If it is acute it will be less than 90° and if it is obtuse it will be more than 90°.*

# Question cracker

Measure these angles in degrees:

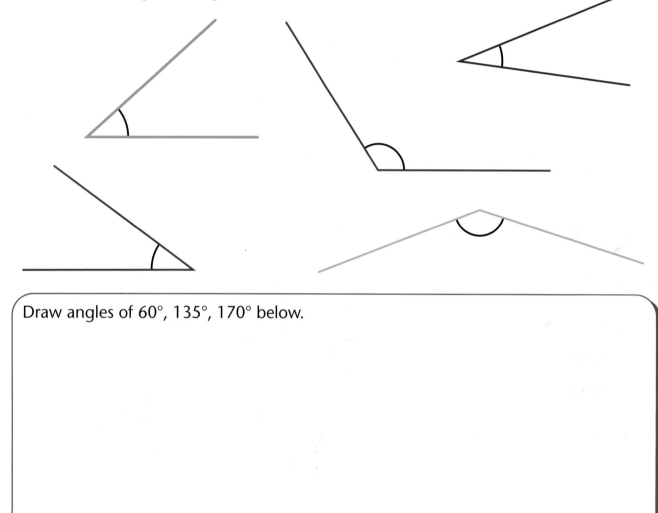

Draw angles of 60°, 135°, 170° below.

Top tip!

*A turn of two right angles, or 180°, is sometimes called a straight angle or a straight line angle.*

### Talking Points

It's time to look at time. There are two types of clock, digital and analogue.
Digital clocks can be 12 hour or 24 hour.

**12 hour digital**

**24 hour digital**

**analogue**

Work with a friend to give each other a time, such as 4:55 p.m.,
and say, write or draw it in different ways.

★ Use **a.m.** for times between midnight and midday, and **p.m.** for
times between midday and midnight.

★ Use 24 hour clocks. Count on past midday, so 1 p.m. becomes 13:00,
2 p.m. becomes 14:00 and so on. Remember we always use four digits
when writing 24 hour clock times, like these: 13:45, 16:00 and 03:25.

## Let's investigate

This CD shows the playing time of songs.
How long would it take to listen to:

songs 1 and 3? ..................................

songs 2 and 4? ..................................

all the songs? ..................................

Which three songs take exactly 13
minutes to play?

...................................................

...................................................

...................................................

1. HELP ME — 3 MIN 25 SECS
2. DOMINO — 4 MIN 38 SECS
3. MOONDANCE — 4 MIN 30 SECS
4. THAT'S LIFE — 5 MIN 46 SECS
5. SWEET THING — 3 MIN 52 SECS
6. WILD CHILDREN — 3 MIN 09 SECS

1782 589

If there was a 3 second gap between each song and you listened
to the songs in order, which song would be playing after:

12 minutes? ..................     18 minutes? ..................     24 minutes? ..................

Design your own CD with your own song titles. Make up some times for them.
Work out how long it would take to play some of the songs together.

 **Solve it**

You will need a newspaper or TV guide with the times of today's TV programmes. Write what's on these channels at the times shown and how long the programmes are on for.

| BBC2 | 9:15 a.m. |
|---|---|
| ITV | 09:35 |
| Sky 1 | Five to ten in the morning |
| BBC1 | 13:47 |
| CH 4 | Two ten in the afternoon |
| ITV | Quarter to six in the evening |
| CH 5 | 7:25 p.m. |
| MTV | 20.01 |
| BBC1 | Ten fifty at night |
| ITV | 23:30 |

**Facts to learn for Unit Nine**

10 millimetres = 1 centimetre
1000 millimetres = 1 metre
1 kilogram = 1000 grams
$\frac{1}{2}$ litre = 500 millilitres

$\frac{1}{4}$ metre = 25 centimetres

100 centimetres = 1 metre
1000 metres = 1 kilometre
1 litre = 1000 millilitres
$\frac{1}{2}$ kilometre = 500 metres

$\frac{1}{4}$ kilogram = 250 grams

# UNIT NINE  Measurement and Reading Scales

In this unit you will learn:

★ about standard units
★ how to measure accurately
★ about choosing units and instruments to measure with
★ how to read scales accurately.

## Warm up – workout!

*Cover the page opposite!*

Test yourself on the measurements facts from Unit Eight:

10 millimetres = ................................

1000 millimetres = ................................

$\frac{1}{4}$ metre = ................................

1 kilogram = ................................

................................ = 1000 millilitres

................................ = 250 grams

................................ = 1 metre

$\frac{1}{2}$ litre = ................................

................................ = 500 metres

................................ = 1 kilometre

## Talking Points

Colour the cards below so they make three groups:

**1** mass and weight     **2** capacity     **3** length

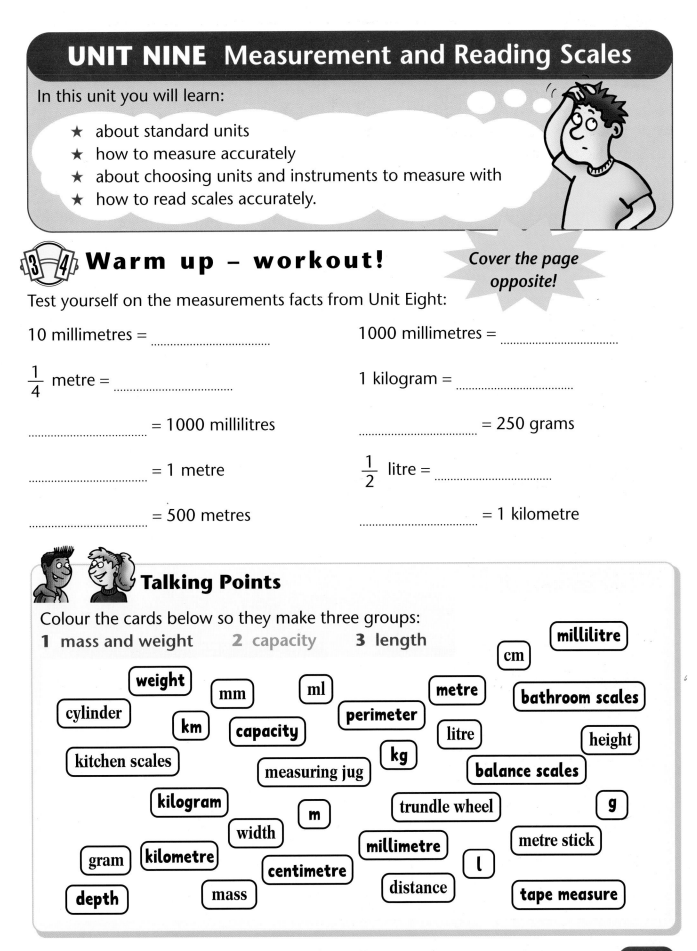

millilitre

cm

weight

mm

ml

metre

bathroom scales

cylinder

km

capacity

perimeter

litre

height

kitchen scales

measuring jug

kg

balance scales

kilogram

m

trundle wheel

g

width

metre stick

gram

kilometre

millimetre

l

depth

centimetre

distance

tape measure

mass

# Word work

Do you know the meaning of all these words? Circle any you think you know.

| centimetre   mass   millimetre   distance |
| depth   kilometre   millilitre   width |
| kilogram   metre   weight   height   litre |
| perimeter   length   gram |

Write the abbreviations for these measurement units:

centimetre ...............     millimetre ...............     gram ...............     litre ...............

millilitre ...............     kilometre ...............     metre ...............     kilogram ...............

## Talking Points

These children are measuring lines.
Can you see what they are doing wrong?
Tick the line that is being measured correctly.
What is the length of the line?

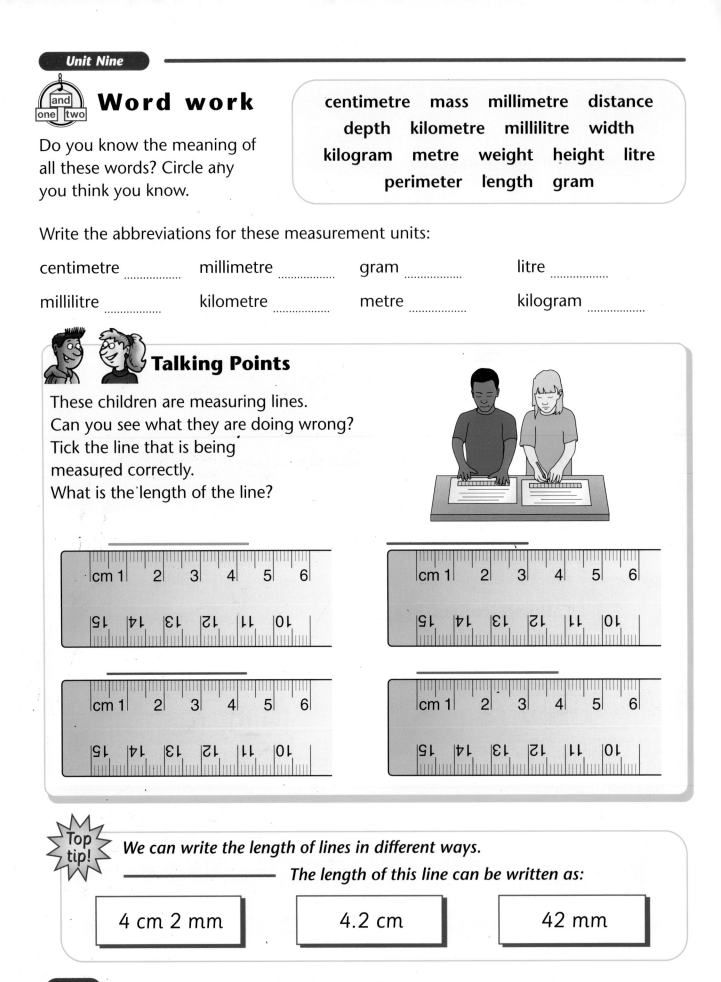

**Top tip!** *We can write the length of lines in different ways.*

*The length of this line can be written as:*

| 4 cm 2 mm | 4.2 cm | 42 mm |

# Question cracker

In the boxes, write the lengths of these objects in three ways.

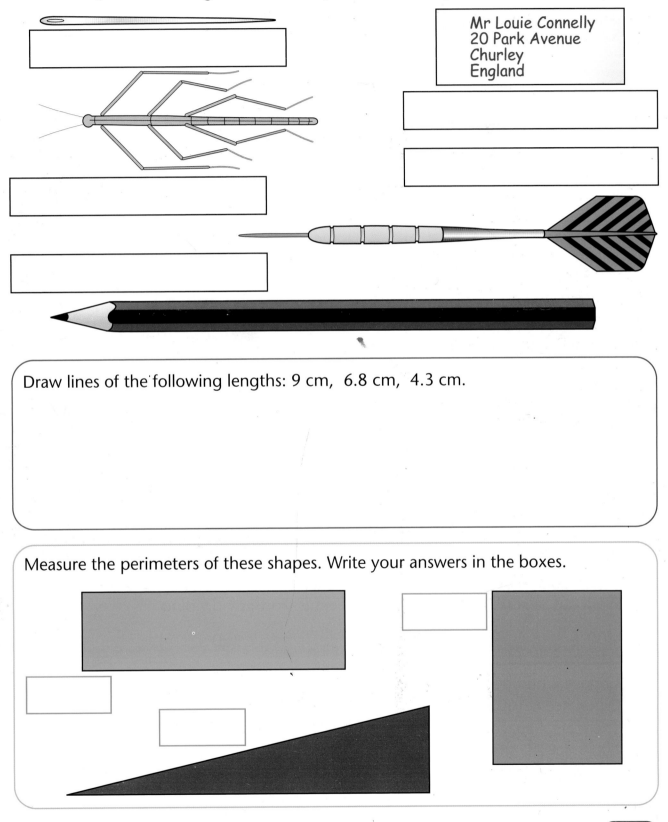

Mr Louie Connelly
20 Park Avenue
Churley
England

Draw lines of the following lengths: 9 cm, 6.8 cm, 4.3 cm.

Measure the perimeters of these shapes. Write your answers in the boxes.

 # Let's investigate

Choose some measuring instruments and use them to measure things in the room. Find things that match the targets below. Measure your items and see how close you can get to each of the targets.

| Target 1 | length 30 cm | sheet of A4 paper | 29.7 cm |
|----------|--------------|-------------------|---------|
| Target 2 | height 1.5 m | | |
| Target 3 | mass  150 g | | |
| Target 4 | capacity 600 ml | | |
| Target 5 | mass  1.3 kg | | |
| Target 6 | capacity  8 l | | |

# Skills builder

Can you see what each scale is showing?

Here's a way of reading scales like these accurately.
1  Choose two numbers that are next to each other on the scale.
2  Find the difference between them.
3  Count how many spaces there are between them.
4  Work out how much each of these spaces is worth by dividing.

```
   600                 700                 800
  |   |   |   |   |   |   |   |   |   |   |
```

1  Choose 2 numbers: 600 and 700.
2  Difference is 100.
3  There are 4 spaces between them.
4  100 ÷ 4 = 25, so each space is worth 25.

Write the correct numbers on each point on the line.

# Question cracker

Write what each scale is showing.

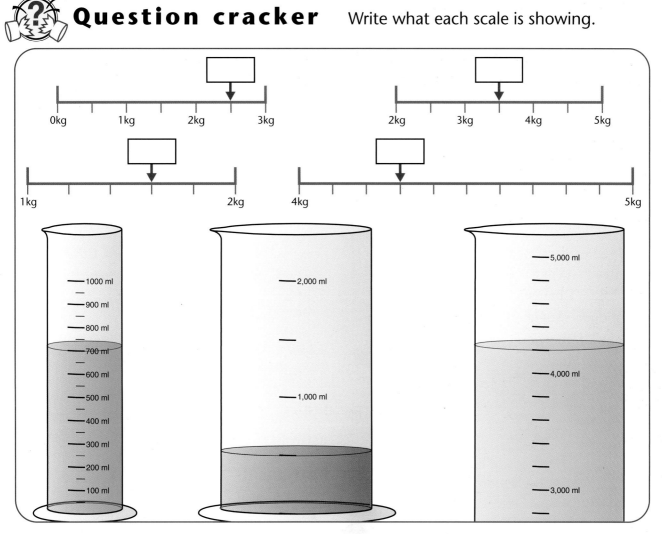

Mark an arrow on the scale to show the reading given.

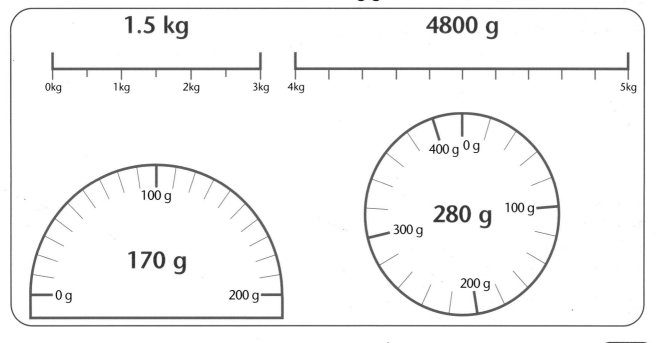

## Solve it

Read these headlines carefully to find a measurement.
Write:
★ what unit you would use to measure it
★ an estimate of its size
★ what instrument you would use to measure it.

Mr Wright arrived at work yesterday with a bandage round his head. He said, 'I banged it on the door frame. The height of the door was less than I thought'.

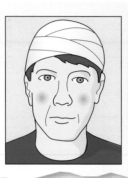

unit: ...................................

estimate: ...................................

instrument: ...................................

**SALE!** *Discount on all school blackboards and whiteboards.*

*Length of classroom board is*

unit: ...................................

estimate: ...................................

instrument: ...................................

Bearwood School said yesterday that they are to get larger waste bins. Mrs Trainer, a teacher, said, 'The capacity of the bins in the classroom isn't big enough for all the rubbish produced by the children.'

unit: ...................................

estimate: ...................................

instrument: ...................................

### 'Year 6 pupils getting bigger!'

A survey showed that the weight of a Year 6 pupil in the year 2000 is likely to be heavier than the weight of a Year 6 pupil in the past. 'I think it's all the burgers and chips,' said Luke, between mouthfuls.

unit: ...................................

estimate: ...................................

instrument: ...................................

### Check before starting Unit Ten

Look over the 'Warm-up – work out' facts you have learnt in other units.

In this unit you will learn:

★ about different kinds of tables and graphs
★ how to read information from graphs and charts
★ about finding the mode and range of data
★ how to carry out an experiment and graph the results.

## Warm up – workout!

Test yourself on these questions from all the other units

$24 + 9 =$ ...................

1 kilometre = ................... metres

$36 \div 6 =$ ...................

$6 \times 7 =$ ...................

................... seconds = $\frac{1}{2}$ minute

$\frac{1}{4}$ of $24 =$ ...................

$40 \times 10 =$ ...................

................... grams = 1 kilogram

$45 - 22 =$ ...................

$90 \times 4 =$ ...................

................... days = 1 normal year

$48 \div 8 =$ ...................

$6200 \div 100 =$ ...................

A ................... has 6 straight sides

## Word work

| survey    bar chart    data    line graph    frequency table |
| tally chart    Carroll diagram    mode    axes |
| Venn diagram    range    axis |

Join the words to the charts with a line.

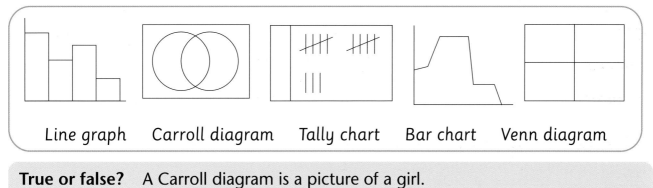

Line graph    Carroll diagram    Tally chart    Bar chart    Venn diagram

**True or false?**   A Carroll diagram is a picture of a girl.

**Top tip!** *The* **mode** *is the most popular or most frequent value.*
*The* **range** *is the difference between the highest and lowest values.*

Make a tally chart of these bowling scores:

**Bowling scoresheet – round 1**

| | | | |
|---|---|---|---|
| David | 5 | Jenny | 7 |
| Sanjay | 8 | Luke | 2 |
| Dan | 5 | Nita | 10 strike! |
| Chloe | 6 | Sam | 6 |
| Neil | 2 | Cath | 8 |
| Ali | 6 | Fiona | 7 |
| Megan | 4 | Alice | 10 strike! |

Tally chart

What is:  the **highest** score? ........................  the **lowest** score? ........................

the **mode** value? ........................  the **range**? ........................

## Skills builder

This survey recorded the ages of people under 30 buying CDs in **Your Price** on Saturday. These are shown in a tally chart.

If we want to draw a bar chart we need to sort the information into groups.
This sketch might help you see why.

Tally chart

| age | | age | |
|---|---|---|---|
| 10 | II | 20 | II |
| 11 | I | 21 | III |
| 12 | I | 22 | I |
| 13 | | 23 | I |
| 14 | II | 24 | |
| 15 | I | 25 | II |
| 16 | II | 26 | I |
| 17 | | 27 | II |
| 18 | HHT | 28 | |
| 19 | | 29 | II |

Age   10  11  12  13  14  15  16  17  18  19  20  21  22  23  24  25  26  27  28  29

To group the information, see how many people are between certain ages, like in this frequency table.
Count up the people and fill in the table.

How many bars will you need to draw on the bar chart now?

| Ages | Total number of people |
|---|---|
| 10 – 14 | ........................ |
| 15 – 19 | ........................ |
| 20 – 24 | ........................ |
| 25 – 29 | ........................ |

Draw a bar chart to show the ages of people under 30 buying CDs on Saturday. Use the **grouped data**.

A bar chart to show ...................................................................................................

# Question cracker

Answer these questions about the bar chart.

| How many people took part in the survey? | |
|---|---|

| In which age group were there fewer than seven people surveyed? | |
|---|---|

| In which two age groups were the same number of CDs bought? | |
|---|---|

| What was the modal group? | |
|---|---|

# Let's investigate

|  | Aberdeen | Birmingham | Cardiff | Exeter | Leeds | Newcastle |
|---|---|---|---|---|---|---|
| Aberdeen | — | 690 | 859 | 946 | 529 | 380 |
| Birmingham | 690 | — | 173 | 261 | 194 | 336 |
| Cardiff | 859 | 173 | — | 196 | 385 | 515 |
| Exeter | 946 | 261 | 196 | — | 471 | 601 |
| Leeds | 529 | 194 | 385 | 471 | — | 155 |
| Newcastle | 380 | 336 | 515 | 601 | 155 | — |

**JULY**

| S | M | T | W | T | F | S |
|---|---|---|---|---|---|---|
|  |  |  |  |  |  | 1 |
| 2 | 3 | 4 | 5 | 6 | 7 | 8 |
| 9 | 10 | 11 | 12 | 13 | 14 | 15 |
| 16 | 17 | 18 | 19 | 20 | 21 | 22 |
| 23 | 24 | 25 | 26 | 27 | 28 | 29 |
| 30 | 31 |  |  |  |  |  |

**Bus 44**

| | | |
|---|---|---|
| Town centre | 08:35 | 12:45 |
| Leisure centre | 08:40 | 12:50 |
| Hospital | 08:55 | 13:05 |
| Library | 09:00 | 13:10 |
| Pool | 09:17 | 13:27 |

## CBA cinemas

Films showing at:

| | | |
|---|---|---|
| **12:00** | **13:45** | **15:10** |
| **19:00** | **20:45** | **22:10** |

Write three statements about each of the tables above.

_____

_____

_____

_____

_____

_____

_____

_____

_____

_____

_____

_____

# Solve it

A prisoner has escaped from jail, wearing an electronic tag.
The police can track how many kilometres he is from the prison.
This **line graph** shows the prisoner's movements during the morning.

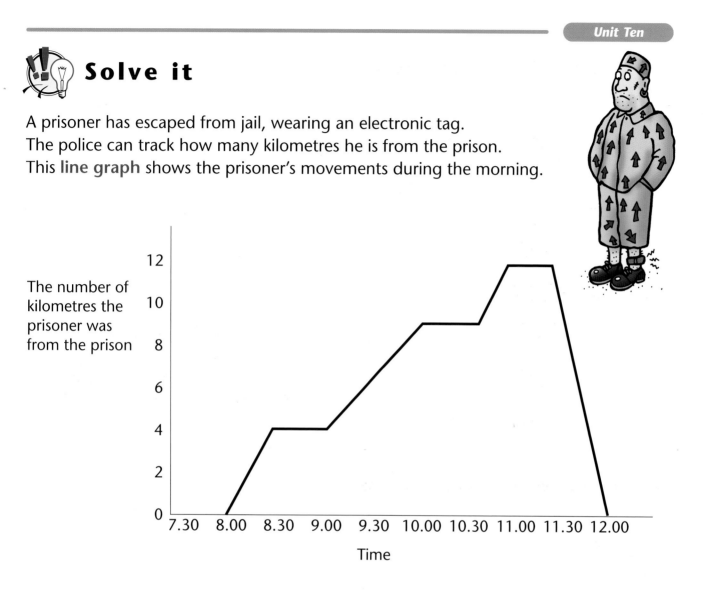

The number of kilometres the prisoner was from the prison

Time

With a friend, answer these questions about the line graph.

**What time did the prisoner escape?**

_____

**How far did he travel in the first half hour?**

_____

**How far from the prison was he at 10.00?**

_____

**What did he do from 10.00 to 10.30?**

_____

**What was the furthest he got from the prison?**

_____

**What time do you think was he caught?**

_____

Make up some more questions to answer about the graph.

# Let's investigate

You will need an elastic band, a ruler, squared paper, a metre stick or tape measure, a protractor, a sheet of card and some space!

Place the protractor as shown and mark all the multiples of 10° to 90° on the card. Extend the lines so they are as long as the ruler.

## What to do

One person holds the card upright on the floor while the other person holds the ruler along the 10° line. Hook the elastic band around the end of the ruler and pull it so it is quite tight. Remember exactly where you pulled it to, such as to the 12 cm mark on the ruler. Now let go! Measure and record how for the band has gone. Now repeat for 20°, 30° and so on.

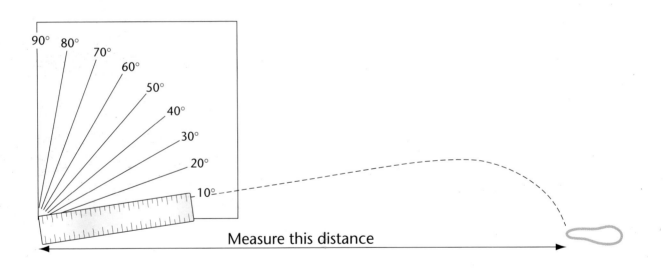

Measure this distance

Record your measurements in a table and then draw a graph of the results on graph paper or centimetre – squared paper. Mark the axes as shown.

**Which angle sent the band furthest?** ........................

What does this mean for golfers, javelin throwers and goalkeepers kicking the ball?
Watch them. Is this what they do?